The Adventures of KITTY CAT
The Billion $$ Power Ball Winner, Vol 3

Marching for Democracy: 2018

by

Renee Blanche
Photos by Linda Ozag

The Adventures of KITTY CAT
The Billion $$ Power Ball Winner, Vol 3

Marching for Democracy: 2018

First Edition, November 2018
Copyright (c) 2018 by Renee Blanche

Contact:
ReneeBlanche@aol.com
Printed by CreateSpace,
An Amazon.com Company
Available on Kindle and other book stores
ISBN-13: 978-1729707401
ISBN-10: 1729707408

Dedication
To my mother, Blanche, 97,
Jill, Laura, Mary, Amalia,
Harmony and Cadence

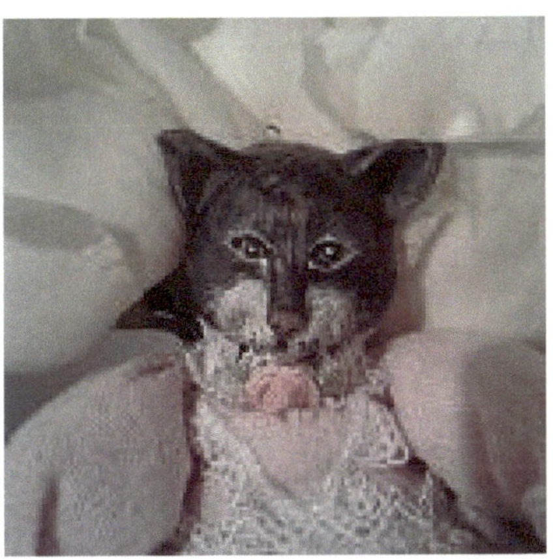

Acknowledgements
With thanks to Margaret Atwood, Sara K, Civia, Carol,
and all the Women Marchers I met
October 13, 2018 in Chicago

EPISODE I

Kitty Cat took the bus to the *March on Chicago*, October 13, 2018. She wore her marcher's pink ruffled dress and traveled with Linda O, the famous photographer, a student of Eliot Porter.

Kitty wasn't sure why she was going to this march. She was still angry, because of the weight she had gained while watching the Senate Hearings all week

on TV that confirmed Brat KeveNo as a
Supreme Court Justice.

She was still angry that her President was
now being called "POTUS," as if she
should know what a "potus" was. Were
people in America not wanting to
associate the name President with the
name, Trumpee?

She was angry that females were still snickered at for being females. It was a chromosome thing, no fault of their own.

So she got on the #151 bus. After all, she had marched in Chicago, January 2017, her first Chicago march. (Grant Park was not really a march.) She marched in New York City, January 2018, maybe in honor of women who marched the year before.

WOMEN'S MARCH 2018
#postcardtuesdays

Then in Chicago, June 30, Kitty Cat
marched to oppose the separation of
children from their parents at the border
of the United States of America. Kitty
heard the Ellis Island ghosts talking to
her.

2,000 Stolen Kids
Cult45 Concentration Camps
being Prepared for People
25,000 - Alabama
47,000 - N. California
47,000 - S. California
#s TBD

I thought
you were
PRO-LIFE?
#ABOLISHICE

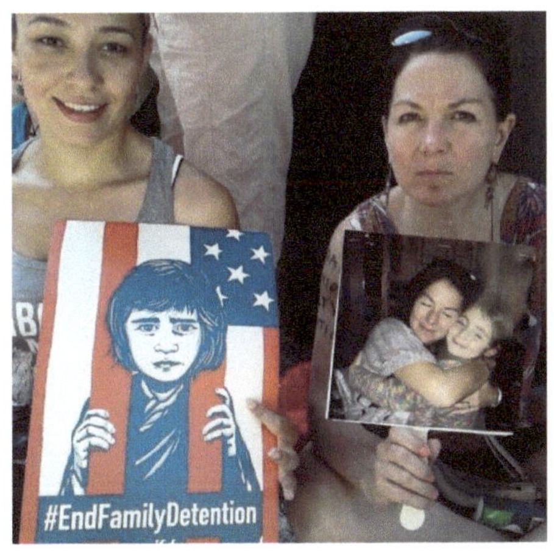

Kitty Cat knew why she was marching then, but this time, she was going mostly because she said she would.

She was already a voter, so she did not need to register. But there were all these signs saying: VOTE!

They starting walking east on Monroe Street from Michigan Avenue, passing the police and a few booths of women and men with signs and buttons and handouts saying do this and do that.

Kitty gathered up the literature, noting that some of the Millennials had probably written some of the content, especially: "Stop this shit."

Kitty did not remember reading the word, *shit*, on political literature before, but it did make her laugh, and surprisingly, relax.

Irreverence has its place in combating injustice.

Kitty passed a man she thought she had seen on TV behind Trumpee. He had on a USA T-Shirt, and was very stoic and scary enough that after Kitty asked, "May

I take your picture?" and the man
nodded, Kitty scurried away.

The rally was starting and the singers on
stage, named Serendipity, were really

good, and Kitty almost wished she was
dancing somewhere, but then she
remembered why she was there. She
was there to find out why she was there.

They passed a small group of people
dressed in black. Really creepy, Kitty
thought. The men had long beards.

That wasn't creepy. What was creepy
were the dozen of women and young
girls who were wearing long black skirts,
black hose, black shoes (nice shoes, Kitty
thought, solid and shiny), black jackets,
black hats.
Hmmmm   Hmmmm

She was reminded of *The Crucible*.
Hmmm. Kitty had sat in front of Arthur
Miller, years before at his opening of the
opera, *A View from the Bridge*. She
wondered if Arthur would think these
people in black reminded him of the
characters in his play.

Was Kitty showing a bias? Had she seen
too many TV shows about polygamists
who used girls as sex slaves. Were these
people demonstrating for their equality?
Kitty looked at the young girl wearing all
black. Did she have a choice to wear a
pink ruffled dress, if she wanted to wear
one?
Hmmmm

EPISODE II

When Kitty saw the Trumpee balloons, she wasn't sure what they were at first. Then she saw the giant baby blimp. It did look like her president. She had given up believing he might be a good president when he maligned the press. Kitty had seen *Enemy of the People*. Did Trumpee know that the "Enemy" was Ibsen's hero?

Certainly, Kitty had not been happy with CNN's arguments, louder and louder, before the election. Kitty preferred listening to C-SPAN. (Sometimes she would fall asleep to the panel discussions of her Congressmen and Senators interviewing all sorts of people.)

After the election, however, after the racist, anti-Semitic, and homophobic remarks were cheered at by Trumpee's supporters, Kitty wondered who those cheerers were.

Were these the cheers of strangers in 1939 Germany?

Kitty had always taken being an American for granted. It was easy to Meow whenever she felt she needed to

Meow. But what if she were being
followed by a pack of dogs down an
alley? Would she hide? Would she
fight?

Kitty knew that she had to listen more,
not just to C-SPAN, CNN, MSNBC, but
also to FOX, which had Frat Boys and
Stepford Wife moderators who hated
everyone Kitty admired as being smart
and well-meaning.

As Kitty walked, she started to talk to the
people in the crowd. There were lots of
people at the rally:

There were people in front of and behind the line of booths along the Grant Park road leading away from the rally.

Each booth supported a new politician.
Paul Vallas was running. Toni Preckwinkle
was running. Kitty knew their records
and signed their petitions.

Then Kitty was approached by a young
man: "Will you sign my petition to allow
. . . (someone Kitty did not know) . . . to
run for Congress?"

Kitty was puzzled. Would she sign the
petition? Someone wanted her to
commit. He wanted her to commit her
signature, not her vote, but her signature
to allow this person to run for office.
The person's name was Hispanic.

"Does she support Planned Parenthood?"
Kitty knew that she believed in a
female's right to determine her own

destiny, to control what happens to her body. Kitty was as surprised at her question as the man holding the petition. "Yes, she is a supporter . . . "
Kitty signed.

As she walked away, she thought: I know why I am here. I'm here to find out what I believe, for what I will fight, and to support those who will fight for the values that my Democracy--as I see it--supports.

Kitty believed in unions and public education. She believed that borders to the United States should stay open to the people of the world who needed sanctuary.

Kitty had traveled through many states, and she had seen the empty land where millions more could live and thrive. I bet, Kitty thought, if you moved all of Yemen to Nevada or Kansas or places in Illinois, no one would even miss the land.

 The Trumpets were always talking, yelling, screaming about others: "Look at that bad Liberal," they would say. "A Liberal wants to kill you."

 Kitty was a billionaire, and she knew that many of her fellow billionaires were using those Trumpet FoxLovers to distract them from seeing: A true billionaire got that way from taking from someone else who was not looking or thinking. (Except Kitty, of course, who had won her money playing the lottery.)

Yep, Kitty thought, I like Democracy. I don't like autocrats. I don't like oligarchs. From all her C-SPAN watching she was finally learning what the words meant. She understood she did not like men who had power over her. Men on the street. Men on TV. Men in government.

Kitty also did not like women who followed men like little puppies.

Kitty signed several petitions as she walked past those booths. She met Bill Daley, who was thinking about running for mayor. He walked so fast, though, that Kitty did not get the chance to ask him, if he was for Planned Parenthood.

Then a tiny, very sweet young woman asked Kitty to sign a petition for someone named Dorothy.

Kitty asked: "Is she for Planned Parenthood?"

The little woman said, "Well, she is against a woman having to end her baby's life."

"You mean she is for the government controlling a woman's body?" Kitty was surprised she was so rude to this sweet-looking woman. Hmmmm
When did what she _believe_, trump what she _felt_?

"Well, I don't know, but I am against abortion," the woman said.

Kitty looked at this sweet face and said: "If the person who votes to end Roe vs Wade promises to raise the child of any woman who is denied an abortion, I might respect that person. What if a girl is raped? Will you raise that girl's child?"

"Society will place those children in homes and . . . "

Kitty remembered the children she had known who told her of the group and foster homes where they had been raised. Kitty, too, had grown up on the streets, not always a safe place to spend a lifetime.

Kitty felt like being nice, but her mouth could not stop: "What about if a female will die unless she aborts? Who makes that decision?"

That sweet face was now cringing. Kitty wanted to say to that sweet cringing face: "Hypocrite," but she didn't.

Then, the sweet-faced woman's face turned mean, but still controlled, because she wanted Kitty's signature. "Will you sign?"

Kitty walked away. Was she as angry as she felt? Was she giving away her signature too easily?

Voting was not easy. Voting meant having to think. What was right; what wrong? What do I believe? What are my values? What do I stand for? What am I prepared to fight for? What am I prepared to sacrifice?

Yep, Democracy was trapped somewhere in those questions.

Kitty did not have all the answers. But she was marching to discover them. She was marching for her Democracy.

VOTE
ACLU Voter
VOTE LIKE YOUR RIGHTS DEPEND ON IT.
ACLU Illinois

JUST VOTE BLUE

EPISODE III

Kitty checked her watch. Hmmmm. She was ready to leave. So was her photographer, Linda, who was taking so many pictures. Kitty took a few more photos herself, and then the two started walking towards the #151 Bus.

They saw a woman carrying a half pound bag of Intelligentsia coffee and were unhappy to discover that the coffee was a free sample. "Hmmmm," they said, "How did we overlook that?"

"Should we take a cab?" Kitty asked, knowing Linda's answer. (Linda liked buses.) Linda gave Kitty the "Of course not" look.

On the bus home, sitting on the back section, where Kitty had not sat before, they watched the hundreds of people in Chicago who were shopping, and going to movies, or maybe to Lincoln Park Zoo. These people had not been to the march. Would they vote? Do they see Democracy slipping away?

Kitty did not know until Trumpee was elected how much she enjoyed being an American. Traveling the world, she had been shy to say where she was from. Americans were bossy, noisy, superior but well-meaning.

What were they now? Were Americans willing to fight for the right to protest? Would there be a time when marching was outlawed.

Trumpee was elected. People voted for him. We did it--to ourselves. We wanted a TV life and now we have it: Slick and scheming, without the popcorn.

On November 6, 2018, Kitty voted with 114 million other Americans. Not all voted for Kitty's favorites, but that was all right. Many voted for Kitty's justice.

Kitty was learning why she was marching, why she was fighting for Democracy.

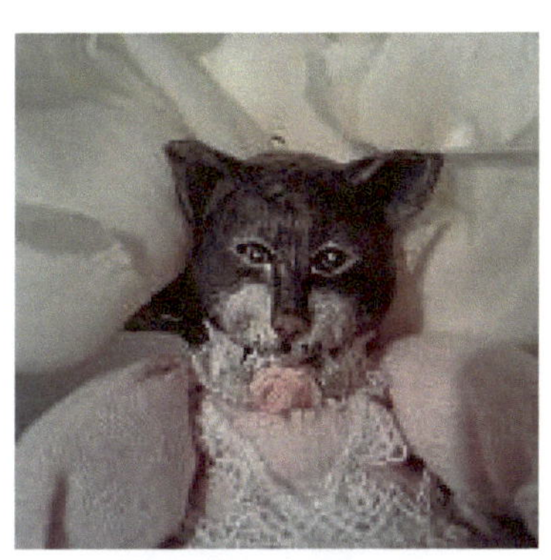

THE END
ReneeBlanche@aol.com

And a New Beginning

TIPS TO MARCHING

1. PACK ONLY YOUR ESSENTIAL NEEDS

2. PACK A SNACK

3. CHARGE YOUR PHONE AT HOME

4. WEAR LAYERS

5. WEAR COMFORTABLE WALKING SHOES

6. CHECK ONLINE REGULARLY FOR EXACT LOCATIONS, TRANSPORTATION, AND TIME CHANGES.

7. TRAVEL WITH A FRIEND FROM HOME

8. ONCE THE CROWDS FORM, YOU NEED A BACKUP PLAN WHEN YOU CANNOT FIND YOUR OTHER FRIENDS (Phone service may not work in a large crowd.)

9. BE COURAGEOUS

10. BE A PEACE MARCHER

ACTIVIST'S GUIDE

1. Find websites that speak to you.
(Be aware that you may not agree with all of their positions.) You will learn, however, details about your specific cause and how to fight for that cause. (See ACLU, CREDO Action and Elizabeth Warren's online petitions below as examples of websites, groups, and individuals advocating for women's rights.)
2. C-SPAN is a 24 hour/daily primary source for most of the news channels. It may make you sleepy at first, but you will hear exactly what your Senators and Representatives say and not a newscaster's shortened, opinionated version. They also feature call-in shows asking for your opinion (and opponents' opinions). And there are no commercial breaks on C-Span.
3. Listen to the other side, and find ways to communicate with those who do not agree with you.

FACEBOOK COMMENTS ABOUT THE MARCH

Thank you everyone for a strong dose of empowerment and hope for the future.

I am so glad I went, it was like therapy for my soul. I was already highly distressed with the state of the Gov't., but the 2 wks. of kavanaugh nearly put me over the edge. It was about so much more than him. I felt dismissed as a woman and more. The rally and march renewed me. energized me, gave me more hope! The like-minded energy was amazing! Thank you to the organizers and everyone involved!

That is what democracy looks like!!

The fiscal performance is at odds with what President Trump promised on the campaign trail, when he said he would eliminate the debt over two terms. Fiscal 2018 was the first full fiscal year under Trump's watch, and debt has risen from $20 trillion to around $21.5 trillion since he took office.

So I have a couple of people ask me what Saturday was all about, I told them this: the importance of the March to the Polls is that we turned anger and outrage in something positive, very positive. Outrage can take you down a number of paths, most of them destructive to one's being and one's community. What I saw yesterday is that people are engaged, dedicated and very willing to be their own heroes. What WMC's March to the Polls does is amplify the power of one into the power of the many. Together we are the hope, we are the power to transform emotion into action. We are the connection that this world so desperately needs. We are the people, we are the network of people that will make positive change happen and we are the ones who will here for the long haul down that road of justice.

MUELLER FIRING PROTESTS

Here's a message from the host of the Mueller Firing Rapid Response event you signed up to attend:

Reminder: TONIGHT we meet at Federal Plaza at 5pm to demand that Matthew Whitaker recuse himself from the Mueller investigation. When Rod Rosenstein was removed from the Mueller investigation, a Red Line was crossed and so we take the streets.

Please bring homemade signs and dress appropriately for the weather. This is just the beginning. We are faced with a constitutional crisis and must continue to take action and ensure the Trump Administration is held accountable. To make sure you are part of all future actions, please join Indivisible Chicago for daily actions you can take to resist the Trump and GOP agenda. Go to www.indivisiblechicago.com and join up now.

Please let us know you are going on Facebook and share the event https://www.facebook.com/events/1807428685983766/

Congress has the constitutional authority and obligation to hold Trump accountable for this abuse of power. But we've seen the Republican Congress give Trump pass after pass every time he crosses another line.

If this isn't the moment when Congress puts country over party to hold Trump accountable, it's not clear whether it will ever happen. Let's show our lawmakers that we won't stand by while they allow Trump to slide the United States into authoritarianism.

When Richard Nixon fired Archibald Cox from the Watergate investigation, it became a tipping-point moment for lawmakers in his own party to finally decide that they had to act or risk forfeiting our democracy. It's up to us to make Trump's appointment of Whitaker into the moment when our lawmakers finally wake up and prevent Trump from putting himself above the law.

You can reply to this email by visiting your event dashboard here: https://act.moveon.org/event/mueller-firing-rapid-response-events/13278/attend/?akid=.7544414.gvABQ_

You're receiving this message because you're signed up for an event. You can use your event tools, linked above, to cancel your signup and quit receiving these messages.

ENSURE THAT ILLINOIS ALLOWS FULL ACCESS TO REPRODUCTIVE HEALTH CARE

SUPPORT HB 40

Sponsors: Feigenholtz

For more information contact:
Khadine Bennett: 312.607.3355
kbennett@aclu-il.org
or Brigid Leahy: 217.
553.8976 brigidl@ppil.org

House Bill 40 strikes a dangerous "trigger" provision
in the Illinois abortion law and affirms that Illinois
will not go back to the pre-Roe days of illegal abortion.
.

By removing the anti-choice "trigger" language from the 1975 Act, HB 40 ensures that women's health care
will be protected in Illinois, regardl
ess of what happens to the Supreme
Court in a Trump administration.
There is simply too much risk.
HB 40 removes discriminatory provisi
ons from Illinois law that deny insu
rance coverage of abortion to
many women who depend on Medicaid and State Employee Health Insurance.
Every woman, regardless of whether she has private or
government-funded health insurance, should have
affordable and comprehensive health care coverage that
includes coverage for abort
ion care, so she can make
personal health decisions based on what
is best for her and her family.
State Employee Health Insurance
.

Aside from a narrow life exception, Illinois law bans abo
rtion coverage from non-contributory (employers
cover 100 percent of the premium paym
ents) state employee health plans.
.

Under current policy, state employees and their depend
ents are often denied coverage for reproductive
health care that is commonly available to those who
get their insurance in the private sector, including
denials of coverage for medically necessary abortions or
those required because of lethal fetal anomalies
Medicaid
.

Medicaid has restricted the use of
federal funds for abortion coverage to

cases of life endangerment, rape
or incest under what is known as the "Henry Hyde Am
endment." Under this policy,
health care providers are
often deterred from taking Medicaid as a form of
payment, because of the confusing web of exceptions
and restrictions that apply.
.

The "Henry Hyde Amendment" is not good policy.
Health programs for women with low incomes should
cover birth control, childbirth AND abortion care. All
women, regardless of income should have the same
right to decide if and when to have children.
.

Illinois should join the 15 states
1
that use state funds to provide wome
n with health assistance funds that
cover the full range of pregnancy-related care, includin
g a woman's decision to en
d a pregnancy. In this
time of budget crisis, it is important to note that
this bill would have zero cost for the Department of
Healthcare and Family Services (DHFS).
HB 40 respects that individuals and their fam
ilies need to make their own life decisions
When it comes to the most important decisions in life, like
whether to become a parent, it is vital that a woman is
able to consider all the options available to her. It is no
t our place to interfere with her decision by withholding
coverage. HB 40 is common sense policy that suppo
rts a woman's personal health care decisions.
1
These 15 states have policies t
hat allow state Medicaid funds to cover abortion
services: AK, CA, CT, HI, MD, MA, MN, MI, NJ,
NM,
NY, OR, VT, WA, WV.

ENSURE THAT ILLINOIS ALLOWS FULL ACCESS TO REPRODUCTIVE HEALTH CARE

SUPPORT HB 40

Sponsors: Feigenholtz
For more information contact:
Khadine Bennett: 312.607.3355
kbennett@aclu-il.org
or Brigid Leahy: 217.
553.8976 brigidl@ppil.

ENSURE THAT ILLINOIS ALLOWS FULL ACCESS TO REPRODUCTIVE HEALTH CARE

SUPPORT HB 40

Sponsors: Feigenholtz
For more information contact:
Khadine Bennett: 312.607.3355
kbennett@aclu-il.org
or Brigid Leahy: 217.
553.8976 brigidl@ppil.org

SUPPORTING ORGANIZATIONS

ACLU of Illinois
American Association
of University Women
Chicago Foundation for Women
Equality Illinois
EverThrive Illinois
Illinois Caucus for Adolescent Health
Illinois NOW
McHenry County Citizens for Choice
Mujeres Latinas en Accion
National Council of Jewish Women Illinois State Policy
Advocacy Network
Personal PAC
Planned Parenthood of Illinois

About CREDO Action

CREDO Action organizes for progressive change. We mobilize our 5 million activists to speak out and pressure decision-makers from the local to the national level. From opposing war, to relentlessly defending reproductive freedom, protecting our environment and a healthy food system, fixing our broken democracy, fighting for an economy that works for everyone, and more, CREDO empowers activists to work for the change we want to see, not what we are told we can achieve by Washington insiders.

CREDO Action is the activism arm of CREDO, a social change organization that offers products — like CREDO Mobile — in order to fund grassroots activism and progressive nonprofit organizations.

Over the course of our history, CREDO has donated over $82 million to Democracy Now!, Brennan Center for Justice, Doctors Without Borders, ACLU, EFF, Planned Parenthood, 350.org and hundreds of other nonprofit groups.

Our customers and activists have generated over 16 million letters and phone calls to elected officials, decision-makers and corporate headquarters across the country. Our activists have submitted their signatures over 137 million times on CREDO petitions and in public comments to government agencies.

We believe in the power of people coming together to make real
change — no matter the odds. When we do, we can win.
Our activists have helped win historic victories for peace with
Iran, real Net Neutrality, blocking the Keystone XL pipeline,
Arctic offshore drilling and coal leasing on federal lands, raising
the minimum wage, and blocking Wall Street cronies from
political appointments — and that's just in the last couple of
years.

https://www.warren.senate.gov

from Credo

Stand with Sen. Warren: Make Trump disclose and divest

—Meaningless.‖ That's how the director of the Office of Government Ethics described Donald Trump's recently announced plan to hold on to his business and ownership in hundreds of businesses with billions in assets and more than $600 million in debt.1 It is now more important than ever to get behind Sen. Elizabeth Warren and the group of senate Democrats who have introduced a powerful new presidential conflicts of interest bill.2

With Trump's deep business ties to foreign governments and businesses, he will be in violation of the Constitution's rules against bribery on his first day in

office. But federal conflict-of-interest rules contain a glaring loophole exempting the president and vice president from many restrictions. Sen. Warren's new bill would make it clear that Trump has to follow the rules – or else.3
A president using his power to enrich himself while indebted to foreign governments is not normal, and we cannot let Washington Democrats and the corporate media pretend it is. We need to get behind leaders like Sen. Warren and make it clear that Donald Trump is putting America's safety and security at risk in order to line his own pockets.
The federal watchdog's remarks on Trump's plan have Republicans talking about investigating or defunding his office.4 It isn't the first time. The very first act of the new Republican Congress was an attempt to gut a similar independent office covering Congress, the Office of Congressional Ethics. But under massive public pressure, Republicans changed course within 24 hours. The whole episode was evidence that Trump Republicans are desperate to make corruption easier – and extremely vulnerable to public outrage on this exact issue.
Every modern president has voluntarily chosen to follow conflict-of-interest rules – until now. Even though those rules exempt the president and vice president, past leaders of both parties have divested their financial interests or placed them in a blind trust.5 Trump merely intends to turn over day-to-day operations to his two

sons while maintaining a financial stake in his business, which a bipartisan group of ethicists and good government groups has condemned.6

Trump's refusal to disclose and divest shows that he is intent on enriching himself and his Wall Street friends at the expense of Americans who struggle to make ends meet. This is the type of cronyism and corruption that conflict-of-interest rules are designed to prevent. Worse, his deep business ties to global financiers and the likes of China, Russia, Libya and Turkey put us all at risk. Trump has every incentive to make foreign policy decisions that benefit himself while putting American lives at risk.

Sen. Warren's new bill tackles Trump's potential corruption on both fronts. It would close the loophole allowing the president, vice president and their families to avoid conflict-of-interest rules – forcing Trump to disclose and fully divest his financial interests. It also emphasizes that the anti-bribery —emoluments clausell of the Constitution applies directly to situations like this, where the president's wealth is dependent upon pleasing foreign dictators.7 This bill makes it absolutely clear that Trump's business ties put America at risk, so we need to get behind it in a big way.

Stand with Sen. Warren: Make Trump disclose and divest. Thank you for speaking out.

http://chicagonow.org/new-stuff

Chicago NOW has five key issue teams that are dedicated to making our city a better place for women and girls. If you are interested in getting involved with the CNOW Action Team, email us at **chicagonow.org@gmail.com**. Our core issues are:

 Reproductive Rights

 Economic Equity

 Stop Violence Against Women

 LGBTQ Rights

 Women's Health